FORGOTTEN ARCHIVES 3

THE LOST SIGNAL CORPS PHOTOS

DARREN NEELY

To the Pytchley Crew, you know who you are

Published in 2020 by Panzerwrecks Limited

Design by Lee Archer
Colour artwork by Felipe Rodna
Printed by Finidr. s.r.o.

Website www.panzerwrecks.com

Panzerwrecks Limited
Great Priors
Church Street
Old Heathfield
Sussex TN21 9AJ
United Kingdom
lee@panzerwrecks.com

CONTENTS

INTRODUCTION

Almost six years ago, I came up with the idea for a book to showcase rare and unseen photographs from the US Army Signal Corps collection. The first volume of Forgotten Archives: The Lost Signal Corps photos was published in 2015. Soon after, I was fortunate to meet the families of several Signal Corps cameramen, which led to the publication of a second volume in 2017.

Since then, I have been fortunate to make contact with more families of these brave men. Also, I have continued to scour collections at universities, small colleges, and government archives, which continue to provide Signal Corps photos. In many cases, these collections are not from the photographers, but the men who worked in processing, developing, and selection. One can only manage the number of copies made and stacks of photos available for soldiers to take as a souvenir.

It is the relationships with cameramen's families and the discovery of more photo collections that has enabled me to present this third volume of Forgotten Archives, and the book continues the work of the previous two. Photos are generally presented in chronological order unless on a specific cameraman or topic. There are some instances of using previously seen photos, but only when they have been available in low quality, or I have found additional images.

Where possible, each image is credited to the cameraman, unit, and the original caption is included. These original captions are usually full of misspelled European towns and misidentified units. Sometimes a caption can be as general as '1st Army' or as specific as 'Company D, 1st Battalion, 32nd Armored Regiment, 3rd Armored Division'. Once the photos are classified for use, painstaking research is undertaken to correctly identify the unit, location, and sometimes even the exact date. The official caption is presented in black and my notes and additional information in gray italics.

For this book, I was allowed access to almost all the photos taken by Sgt. Joseph DeMarco of the 165th Signal Photographic. Sgt. DeMarco was the still cameraman with Detachment K of the 165th, his motion picture partner being Leon Rosenmann. Rosenmann would go on to film the capture of Cologne, amongst other events. Detachment K served with the 3rd Armored Division for the duration of the war, and their coverage is a visual history of this famous unit. Sgt. DeMarco left the unit immediately after recording the survivors of TF Hogan in their escape from behind German lines at the beginning of the Battle of the Bulge. His best photos from the unit's first action in July 1944 in Normandy, through the early days of the Bulge, are shown here for your enjoyment.

As ever, I extend my deepest gratitude to all those who helped with caption analysis and writing, vehicle identification, and expertise in different engagements in the ETO. A massive thanks to Lee Archer, my publisher, who keeps my eye on the ball and pushes me along, and to the following experts: Kurt Laughlin, Bill Warnock, Dieter Laes, Eddy Monfort, Timm Haasler, Stephane Cazenave, Dan Fong, Martin Block, Hilary Doyle, and Simon Vosters. My dear friend, Roddy MacDougall, my co-author on Nürnberg's Panzer Factory, unfortunately passed away in 2018. Roddy was quite simply *the* expert on Panther tanks; his help and guidance with my work is sorely missed. My sincere thanks to the Archive of Modern Conflict for the use of their photographs.

Andrew Woods from the First Infantry Division in Illinois was beyond helpful in finding Signal Corps photos. Also, I must thank the following children of US Army Signal Corps cameramen: Norman Shub (Murray Shub and Robert Runyan), Joe & Rick DeMarco (Joseph DeMarco), and Jim & Lisa McAleer and John & Jon McAleer (daughters of Warren Rothenberger).

Once again, Felipe Rodna has done an outstanding job of bringing some of the photos to life with his unrivaled artwork. Kudos, and thank you Felipe!

Thanks again to my wonderful wife Debbie and children Annie and Aidan for continuing to put up with their favorite tank nerd and being patient as I scanned into the wee hours and 'ditched' them for trips to the archives.

Darren Neely, Annapolis, MD, May 2020.

ITALY
Signal Corps Coverage in the Mediterranean Theater

July 25, 1943.

A Tiger from 3./s.Pz.Abt.504 photographed on Strada Providenciale 11, en route to Niscemi, Sicily. The rear of the turret has taken an anti-tank round that undoubtedly caused casualties to the crew. The tank was subsequently pushed off the road and blown up by US engineers.

Collection of General Isaac D. White, CG of 2nd Armored Division.

A Tiger I from 2./s.Pz.Abt.504 in Sicily. The unit's distinctive rhomboid marking can be seen on the lower front hull and it looks like an explosion has lifted the turret off the hull.

Collection of General Isaac D. White, CG of 2nd Armored Division.

A Pz.Kpfw.IV Ausf.G from Panzer-Division Hermann Göring. The insignia on the trackguard indicates that it is from the 3 Kompanie. Based on the numbering of the photo, it was taken by the 17th Armored Engineer Battalion of the 2nd Armored Division in August 1943.

August 9, 1943. Knocked out Panzer IV. Sicily.

A thoroughly wrecked Pz.Kpfw.IV Ausf.G in Sicily. The photo was possibly taken outside Brolo, and the tank subsequently pushed off the road by US engineers. The unit is likely to have been Pz.Abt.215 of 15.Panzergrenadier-Division. See Panzerwrecks 23 for more photos of this tank.

August 12, 1943 (Grann). American Jeep passing knocked out German equipment near Brolo, Sicily.

A Jeep speeds past a Skoda built Sd.Kfz.11 abandoned outside Brolo, Sicily. The insignia on the Sd.Kfz.11's trackguard is for a towed artillery unit. Three more photos of this halftrack appear in Panzerwrecks 13.

Italy

September 15, 1943 (Potter). German tank being taken for salvage near Persono, Italy.

A US recovery crew prepare to recover a Flammpanzer III. The tank, from the Pz.Flamm-Zug of II.Pz.Rgt.2, 16.Panzer-Division was captured near Persano, southeast of Salerno. The images from the subsequent technical intelligence report were shown in Panzerwrecks 9.

10

September 15, 1943 (Potter). Soldier mounting white flag on German tank being salvaged near Sele River.

Two Flammpanzer IIIs were captured; 'F23' and 'F24'. This is 'F24'.

11

September 19, 1943 (Simmons). Communication wire being laid on captured equipment at Altavilla.

This completely wrecked Sd.Kfz.10 had been towing the 5cm Pak 38 in the background before being knocked out by American forces.

January 1, 1944 (Levine) (3131). 881st Heavy Maintenance Company salvage yards Grosseto, close up of three destroyed tanks.

Three M5A1 Light Tanks sit in a salvage yard behind the front line. The middle and right vehicles were from the 13th Armored Regiment of the 1st Armored Division. The Stuart on the left is so heavily damaged that it is beyond repair.

13

January 1, 1944 (Levine) (3131). 881st Heavy Maintenance Company salvage yards Grosseto, group of burned tanks.

Another view of the salvage yard, this time with a pair of M10 3-inch Gun Motor Carriages and M4 (75) Medium Tanks. The M4 to the right is named 'Dirty Gerty,' making it from 'D' Company of a tank battalion. Salvage yards like this were used to repair lightly damaged vehicles and get them back to the front.

A Bulldozer M1A1 mounted on a Medium Tank M4A1 from the 16th Armored Engineer Battalion, attached to the 1st Armored Division in Italy, on September 12, 1944. The tank's registration number 3058559 is visible on the side, and the turret has a circle painted on, signifying a unit identification. The tank has been painted with a striped camouflage pattern.

15

December 3, 1943. American M-4 tank "Katie Did" plowing through heavy mud and across a ditch along the Italian front. Crew members are: in the turret, L-R, 1st Sgt. Claud Right of Onida, South Dakota, Commander, and Cpl. J. P. Herdeck of Chicago, Ill., Gunner: seated in hatches, L-R, Cpl. Carl M. Temy of Fort White, Florida, Assistant Driver, and Cpl. William A. Kelly of Rockway, N.J., Driver.

This tank was mistakenly identified by the cameraman, as it is a Light Tank M5A1. Based on the markings on the front, it is from the 13th Armored Regiment of the 1st Armored Division. The 13th landed near Naples in November, where Allied units had already carved out a beachhead. Note its interesting camouflage pattern.

September 5, 1944 (Levine) (3131). Staged action, close up of tank after being gutted by fire.

The cameraman has noted that the photo was staged. 'Betty' from 'B' Company, 752nd Tank Battalion, is a Medium Tank M4 (75). At this time, the 752nd were supporting the 85th Infantry Division.

October 19, 1944. (Schmidt) (3131). Crew of Somme IV load 76mm ammunition, they are with the 4th Tank Battalion, 1st Armored Division.

The crew of 'Somme IV,' a Medium Tank M4A3 (76), reload ammunition. Its name, 'Somme IV,' would lead us to believe that the crew are on their fourth tank of the war.

February 18, 1945 (Schmidt) (196). II Corps Area, South African Pretoria Regiment using American tanks as artillery. Passing 105mm ammo down to gunner.

Reloading an Assault Gun M4A3 (105) of the South African Pretoria Regiment. During World War II, the Pretoria Regiment (Princess Alice's Own) was attached to the 11th South African Armoured Brigade, 6th South African Armoured Division.

March 18, 1945 (Getty) (196). 1st Armored Division training school, a tankdozer drives the 4 sections of steel pipe containing explosive charge into dike where it will be blown to open hole in dike.

A good side view of a Medium Tank M4 (75) with improvised bulldozer blade mounting. The soldiers are removing the pipe (a bangalore torpedo) to attach it to the blade for demonstration of blowing up dikes and dirt bunkers.

21

No caption was provided with this photo, just a date of August 28, 1943, meaning this Sturmgeschütz III Ausf.G was knocked out in Sicily. It appears to have been pushed off the road, judging by the tracks riding up over the track horns. Only nine Sturmgeschütze were lost in Sicily; four from III./Pz.Rgt.HG, Pz.Div.HG and five from Pz.Abt.129, 29.Pz.Gren.Div.

May 29, 1944 (Ray) (165). Members of an American tank crew load their vehicle with ammunition at a marshaling area, somewhere in England. 66th Armored Regiment, 2nd Armored Division.

Just days before heading across the English Channel, the crew of 'Hawkeye', a Medium Tank M4 (75) of 'H' Company, 66th Armored Regiment, 2nd Armored Division, prepare their tank for the move to Normandy.

June 29, 1944 (Unsen) (165). C-18 pushes through Allied occupied hedge row to next hedge. This is an infantry and tank problem in France.

C-18 is from 'C' Company, 743rd Tank Battalion. This Medium Tank M4A1 with duplex drive is still fitted with the metal skirt, but without the screens that held up the inflatable material that enabled the tank to float. The after-action report for June 29 states that 3rd Platoon, 'C' Company, 743rd, worked with 120th Infantry on coordination for future actions.

July 1, 1944.

The 744th Tank Battalion was equipped with light tanks. 'Battle-Axe', a Light Tank M5A1 with 'B' Company, has thrown a track or run over a mine, requiring the services of an M1A1 wrecker. It is not clear if the M5A1 in the background is disabled or if it is being used as an 'anchor' to recover 'Batte-Axe'.

◀ July 7, 1944 (Unsen) (165). Infantry troops of the 117th Infantry Regiment, 30th Infantry Division, entering the town of St. Fromand, France.

'C-7' is a Medium Tank M4A1 (75) with duplex drive from the 743rd Tank Battalion. The GIs from the 30th Infantry Division are identifiable by their patches, and at least two of them have vests and extra ammunition. The location is Saint-Fromond.

▶ 8th Tank Battalion, 4th Armored Division, Coutances, France.

Up close with a Light Tank M5A1 and its crew from the 8th Tank Battalion, 4th Armored Division, outside Coutances, France. The crew appear to be receiving mail or a newsletter from the soldiers on the left. The tank would have been from 'D' Company. Note the horseshoe on the horn, next to the headlamp.

◀ July 16, 1944 (Lovell) (165). An infantry unit in the St. Lo sector moves ahead after silencing a German tank in the background. 120th Infantry Regiment, 30th Infantry Division.

A GI from the 120th Infantry Regiment, 30th Infantry Division, trudges along with a bazooka and rifle as Jeeps speed past. A Sturmgeschütz III, probably from Panzer-Lehr-Division, sits at the side of the road. With no casualties, smoke or debris to be seen, it seems likely that the vehicle was abandoned.

▶ July 21, 1944 (Horton) (166). Members of the 708th Ordnance Company, 5th Infantry Division, fasten the plow edges to the tank to be used in plowing through hedges.

The 735th Tank Battalion was attached to the 5th Infantry Division at this time. According to the AAR, tanks were sent back to ordnance starting July 17 for the installation of hedgerow cutters. This heavily sandbagged Light Tank M5A1 would have been from 'D' Company. Another waits in the background.

July 27, 1944 (Runyan) (165). A US tank bulldozer passes a knocked-out German tank on its way to assault a German strongpoint in France. 4th Division sector.

Runyan was with the 4th Infantry Division at this time, but this Medium Dozer Tank M4 has the markings of the 610th Light Engineer Battalion. The knocked-out Jagdpanzer IV probably belonged to Pz.Jg.Lehr.Abt.130 of Panzer-Lehr-Division.

July 27, 1944 (Kaye) (165). German prisoners of war walk past a captured Nazi 'Tiger Tank' on their way to a regimental PW stockade near the front lines somewhere in France. 117th Infantry Regiment.

The 'Tiger' is a Pz.Kpfw.IV from 5./Pz.Lehr.Rgt.130. It was knocked out by tanks of the 743rd Tank Battalion and men of the 30th Infantry Division near Le Mesnil-Durand on July 17, 1944. A sign warns curious onlookers about unexploded ordnance and the front left fender has '974' and '7/23/44' chalked on, a sign that the 974th Ordnance Recovery Company has checked it out.

July 30, 1944 (Runyan) (165). Armored infantry aboard halftracks enter Coutances, France.

'C-16', an M3A1 halftrack with the 10th Armored Infantry Battalion, 4th Armored Division, prepares to enter Saint-Sauveur-Lendelin, en route to Coutances, just 10 kilometers away. The driver's name is painted on his armored windshield, as is the next vehicle in line.

August 1, 1944 (Yena) (165). Tankers from an armored unit of E Company, 67th Armored Regiment, reload their machine guns. L to R, Cpl. Robert Rhoads, Sgt. Palmer Richardson, Sgt. Hulon Garner, Sgt. Peter Szabd, Pvt. Melvin Evans, Cpl. Herbert Fredway and Pfc. Frank Kuraswiecz.

The 67th Armored Regiment's AAR for August 1 states that: "The regiment was 1 mile SE of Notre-Dame-de-Cenilly and the day was spent on maintenance, stowage of vehicular loads and rehabilitation of troops." This bunch of soldiers take time to organize MG rounds in front of a Medium Tank M4 named 'Elaine'.

August 8, 1944 (Norbuth) (165). German tank that was knocked out by the 29th Division on the way to Vire, France.

A Sturmgeschütz III or Sturmhaubitze 42 knocked out by the Blue and Grey Division. The vehicle has 'Zimmerit', foliage on the sides and spare roadwheels fitted to the engine deck. Given the condition of the debris on the back of the vehicle, including the helmet, a fire has occurred.

August 9, 1944 (Tomko) (166).

A close-up of the same soldier and smouldering Sd.Kfz.251 was featured in Forgotten Archives 1, page 8. As noted then, the photo is staged, and the wrecked halftrack is probably from 9.Panzer-Division. The GIs are from the 90th Infantry Division.

August 16, 1944 (165). German equipment knocked out in the American drive in the Mortain sector is inspected by Cpl. James R. Jones of Arkansas.

This is a 12 cm Granatwerfer 42; a copy of a Russian regimental mortar. In the background is a captured Pz.Kpfw.IV from 7./SS-Pz.Rgt.1, 1.SS-Panzer-Division, which was in action against the 30th Infantry Division during the Mortain counterattack.

This photo was taken by Joseph Zinni of 166th Signal Photo Company. It did not have a caption and is possibly one that he did not submit for processing. Here, a Panzerspähwagen 204 (f) has a rear axle precariously propped up with bricks and has French graffiti on the back: Vive L'US. In front of the vehicle is what looks like a motion picture camera, and in front of that, the town sign: Carquefou, which is near Nantes, France.

There is no caption for this photo of a Sturmgeschütz IV, somewhere in Normandy. One of the vehicle's toolkits has been removed and now sits opened on the bow armor. The marks on the road indicate that it had been pushed backwards, possibly to clear the road for traffic. The vehicle belonged to SS-Pz.Abt.17 or 2./Pz.Jg.Abt.331.

A Light Armored Car M8 from 'B' Troop, 4th Cavalry Regiment, assigned to the First US Army. Given the environment and soldiers' dress, it is probably from September 1944, maybe Belgium. The M8s were highly mobile and fast, but their thin armor made them vulnerable to medium and heavy weapons. This one has the stars and stripes painted between the driver and assistant driver.

GIs ignore the 'Stay off' signs on this Pz.Kpfw.IV Ausf.J at an ordnance collection point. The style of tactical number and chickenwire on the gun barrel point to the tank being from 6./SS-Pz.Rgt.2 of 2.SS-Panzer-Division, and it was probably lost in July 1944. Note the Sd.Kfz.251 in front of the Panzer.

August 22, 1944 (Cummings) (166). Two knocked out armored vehicles near Ervhille, France.

Two Panzerspähwagen P204 (f) - known as Panhard 178 when in French use. The lead vehicle is smoldering, possibly as a consequence of the shell holes in the front; it is also missing its 25mm cannon. Note the ammunition canisters inside the opened door - for the turret machine gun.

Paris, August 1944. French resistance fighters look over a Sd.Kfz.251 captured from 2.Panzer-Division. The new owners have gone to great lengths to show who now owns it: flags painted on, the French 'Tricolour' fixed to the spare tracks and what looks like an air recognition panel. More photos of this vehicle are on pages 31-33 of Panzerwrecks 15.

August 31, 1944 (Westcott) (165). GIs sit ready at their machine gun for a Nazi patrol moving into range near Seraincourt, France. 60th Infantry Regiment, Co. H.

While his buddy spots his fire with a pair of binoculars, a GI of the 60th Infantry Regiment, 9th Infantry Division, fires at German troops with a Jeep mounted 0·50 Cal machine gun.

A GI poses with a wrecked Pz.Kpfw.IV Ausf.H. The photograph was taken by Milton Marder, a motion picture cameraman assigned to the 166th Signal Photo Company. A chassis number has been painted onto the driver's visor, although unfortunately, it is illegible.

SGT. JOSEPH DEMARCO
165th Signal Photo Company

Sgt. Joseph DeMarco was a still photographer assigned to Detachment K, 165th Signal Photographic Company commanded by Lt Thomas Noble. This unit was attached to the 3rd Armored Division for the duration of the war, and the detachment's photographers can be seen in the 3rd Armored Division Headquarters yearbook. DeMarco was teamed with a motion picture cameraman, T/5 Leon Rosenmann starting in Normandy in mid-June until the end of December when Joe left the unit for medical reasons. His last set of photos were of the infamous "Hogan's lost 400" at Soy, and then he left the unit. DeMarco's photos capture the advance of the 3rd Armored Division through France, into Belgium, the stalemate near the Westwall and the start of the Bulge offensive. A huge thanks to his son Joe Jr. and Rick for allowing access to their Father's photos for use in this book.

▶ *Joe DeMarco in England.*

46

July 7, 1944 (DeMarco) (165). A tank of the 3rd Armored Division passes over a bridge near St. Fromond, France.

'H-34' of 33rd Armored Regiment, 3rd Armored Division, CCB moves over the Vire River as it advances to meet German armored counterattacks. Typical of 33rd tanks, it has the odd contraption below the hull machine gun. Based on the markings, the driver is from Maryland and the assistant driver from Iowa.

July 1944 (DeMarco) (165). Thunderbolts flipped this German tank on its side in a Normandy field.

This Sturmgeschütz IV was from SS-Pz.Abt.17, 17.SS-Panzergrenadier-Division based on the fact that while the photographer gave no location, it is with a batch of photos from the Pont-Hébert area. The vehicle was probably turned onto its roof when pushed from the road.

August 3, 1944 (DeMarco) (165). French refugees returning to Villedieu after its liberation by American forces inspect a German tank that fell victim to American gunners.

This Panzer has been seen before but not at this size and quality. Panther '321', from I./SS-Pz.Rgt.2, 2.SS-Panzer-Division and was lost in Villedieu-les-Poêles. Note that the woman on the far right has a spent shell case in her bag and one of the men is carrying two 7·92mm ammunition boxes. See Panzerwrecks 8 for more photos.

49

August 3, 1944 (DeMarco) (165). German Tiger tank knocked out by American attack on Coutances, France. The top of the turret was completely knocked off.

A Panther from I./Pz.Rgt.6 attached to Panzer-Lehr-Division that was knocked out on the Saint-Lô to Périers road during the intense aerial bombardment that preceded Operation Cobra on July 24th. The force of the explosion has blown the turret completely clear, splitting its side wall.

August 3, 1944 (DeMarco) (165). American maintenance troops remove a blasted Jeep from the road on the way to Villedieu, France.

The wrecker appears to be dropping off a wrecked Jeep at a collection point unless the Medium Tank M4 (75) and Light Armored Car M8 were also knocked out in the area. The tank has the markings of 'F' Company, 33rd Armored Regiment, 3rd Armored Division.

August 13, 1944 (DeMarco) (165). Crewmen of an American tank wave back to the cheering French populace as their tank roars through the streets of Chavaigne in pursuit of the fleeing Germans.

A Medium Tank M4 with a 'Douglas Cutter'; a specific type of hedgerow cutter used by the 3rd Armored Division. The bracket below the hull machine gun is an addition made by the 33rd Armored Regiment

August 13, 1944 (DeMarco) (165). A GI is drinking a glass of wine given to him by French civilians as a US Armored column passes through the town to meet the German resistance.

Following the M4 on the previous page is this M3A1 Halftrack, number 'A-14' of 36th Armored Regiment, being slowed down by civilians offering a glass of wine. Of interest are the ammunition boxes stowed over the driver's compartment, a 0·50 caliber MG up front and water-cooled 0·30 caliber MG at the back.

August 13, 1944 (DeMarco) (165). This armored car knocked out 2 Mark IV tanks with its 37mm gun. They are with the 3rd Armored Division.

This is an excellent shot of a Light Armored Car M8 and crew during a brief period of rest. The armored car belonged to the 32nd Armored Reconnaissance Company of the 3rd Armored Division and carries the name 'Rudy'.

August 14, 1944 (DeMarco) (165). Another member of the Wehrmacht that once overran France lies dead in the back of his armored vehicle when it was stopped by an American shell near Carrouges, France.

Photographed on the outskirts of Carrouges on the edge of the Falaise pocket, a Sd.Kfz.251/11 Fernsprechpanzerwagen. The Sd.Kfz.251/11 was designed as a mobile telephone exchange, and an empty cable reel can be seen on top of the exchange cabinet. Between November 1943 and June 1944, 5% of m.S.P.W. were supposed to be outfitted as Sd.Kfz.251/11. It had a crew of five and was armed with an MG42.

August 26, 1944 (DeMarco) (165). An American tank of the 3rd Armored Division crosses the Seine River at Port Seine on a pontoon bridge erected by engineers.

A Medium Tank M4A1 of the 3rd Armored Division crosses a pontoon treadway bridge. Sandbags have been added to the front, as has a hedgerow cutter. The boat has the markings of 23rd Armored Engineer Battalion, organic to the 3rd Armored Division.

56

October 13, 1944 (DeMarco) (165). Four-man AA gun crew that knocked out one Mark IV tank, one supply truck and killed, wounded and captured 120 Nazi officers and men, and only used 43 shells. 3rd Armored Division.

A great photo of an M15A1 Combination Gun Motor Carriage and crew. Looking at the armament (a 37mm gun with two 0·50 cal machine guns), it is not hard to imagine the destruction they would have inflicted on soft-skinned vehicles. However, the Mark IV kill may have had a degree of luck. These men are with the 486th AAA AW Battalion.

▲ October 14, 1944 (DeMarco) (165). Infantrymen of the 3rd Armored Division, 36th Armored Infantry Regiment, pose with rifles around a Sherman tank near Stolberg, Germany.

A staged photograph for sure. The photo taken immediately before this is one of the most famous of WW2; showing the same soldiers riding on the front of the tank. Clearly, DeMarco asked the men for one photo on the tank and one with two dismounted, their rifles at the ready.

▶ October 25, 1944 (DeMarco) (165). Maintenance Battalion of the 3rd Armored Division installs a transmission in a tank in Walheim, Germany.

A close-up of men from the 3rd Armored Maintenance Battalion fixing the transmission of a Medium Tank M4A1 from 'E' Company, 33rd Armored Regiment.

59

October 25, 1944 (DeMarco) (165). Experiment by engineers with a Sherman tankdozer in covering dragons teeth and paving road over them for other vehicles to pass over.

An interesting idea: instead of blowing up each dragon's tooth, this Medium Bulldozer Tank M4, based on an M4A1, is simply pushing dirt over them to create a ramp. The tank is from the 3rd Armored Division.

November 2, 1944 (DeMarco) (165). During a lull in the activity in Germany, a cow wanders over for a closer look at some M5 light tanks in a field. 3rd Armored Division, Stolberg, Germany.

A platoon of M5A1s from 'C' Company, 32nd Armored Regiment, 3rd Armored Division. The first tank is named 'Comic'.

November 6, 1944 (DeMarco) (165). Adjusting bearings of a motorcycle is T/5 Charles W. Leazer of VT, while rider Pfc. Jack R. Rudeen of MN watches.

An excellent view of a Harley Davidson WLA undergoing some fettling. Note the 0·30 cal ammunition case being used to hold up the bike and nickname 'NO RANK' painted on the fuel tank.

November 19, 1944 (DeMarco) (165). Tank crews of the 3rd Armored Division load their tank to be used as artillery near Mausbach, Germany.

A Medium Tank M4 from 32nd Armored Regiment being used for indirect fire support is reloaded near Mausbach, Germany. Notice the duckboard footpath to ease walking in the mud and spent shell cases in the background.

December 11, 1944 (DeMarco) (165). American armored troops pause for a break in the German town of Langerwehe before moving up to the front. 33rd Armored Regiment, 3rd Armored Division.

Based on after-action reports, these vehicles are probably from 3rd Battalion, 33rd Armored Regiment, TF Hogan of CCR. It is an interesting mix of AFVs; front to back: two Medium Tanks M4, an Assault Tank M4A3E2, another M4, and a 3-Inch Gun Motor Carriage M10.

December 11, 1944 (DeMarco) (165). American soldiers stop to look at two armored vehicles that were put out of action, both the M4 and the TD fell victim to German mines near Langerwehe, Germany. 3rd Armored Division.

This is the next photo in sequence and by judging the road and landscape, probably just up the road. The Medium Tank M4 with command radio set on the glacis is most likely from 'G' Company, 33rd Armored Regiment, 3rd Armored Division, who lost four tanks the previous day. The 90mm Gun Motor Carriage M36 is from 703rd Tank Destroyer Battalion, also attached to the 3rd Armored Division.

◄ December 18, 1944 (DeMarco) (165). Combined roadblock and defense against attack from Luftwaffe are provided by an M5 tank in Germany. Co. C, 33rd Armored Regiment, 3rd Armored Division.

Another view of this Light Tank M5A1 was shown on page 79 of Forgotten Archives 1. Some interesting details are visible here, such as the empty ammunition belt hanging from the 0·30 cal MG, and its tripod mount on the trackguard. The next day, the 33rd Armored Regiment were en route to Belgium.

▶ December 18, 1944 (DeMarco) (165). Watching for planes of Luftwaffe in Germany from their tank top with anti-aircraft MG are Pfc. John Chapman of NH and Sgt. Vernon Johnson of MN with binoculars. Co. C, 33rd Armored Regiment, 3rd Armored Division.

The area is around Stolberg days, if not hours, from the unit being sent to Belgium to defend against the Germans in the VII and XVIII Airborne Corps sector. This Light Tank M5A1 named 'Cake' was photographed on the 18th, and the 33rd Armored was on the move by the 19th at the latest.

September 25, 1944 (Gallo) (166). This American tank was knocked out of action by a direct hit in the fight for Luneville, France.

This Medium Tank M4 was knocked out by an AP shell through the hull side. The tank was from the 749th Tank Battalion, which was attached to the 79th Infantry Division at this time. The AAR states on September 20th that "one tank from 'A' Company was knocked out by a German tank north of Lunéville and was not yet recovered due to enemy artillery fire."

RODNA

October 2, 1944 (Meyer) (166). Cpl. Henry Gillem looks at the damage an 88 shell brought. The 88 pierced the barrel of the 76mm gun of a tank destroyer. 6th Armored Division.

Based on the photo taken after this, we know the area is around Nancy. The turret is from a 76mm Gun Motor Carriage M18 and shows some details, such as the periscope and phone.

October 3, 1944 (Langer) (165). The crew of a 105mm howitzer cleaning their weapon during a lull in the fighting. 434th Armored Field Artillery Battalion, Holland.

The 434th Armored Field Artillery Battalion was organic to the 7th Armored Division, at this time in Holland. Note the large stack of shell casings next to the 105mm Howitzer Motor Carriage M7.

October 5, 1944 (Runyan) (165). T/4 Alfred Lepakowski of Massachusetts, inspects a new radial engine to be put in a Sherman tank attached to a unit fighting in Holland. 31st Tank Battalion, 7th Armored Division.

A Medium Tank M4 gets an engine change; in this case, a Continental R-975. Ordnance units were critical to keeping the tanks operational as they pushed across France, Belgium, Holland and then into Germany.

October 13, 1944 (Bell) (163). GIs ready and stack shells for their 105mm howitzer on their tank. HQ Co., Assault Platoon, 191st Tank Battalion.

The location is Rambervillers in the Vosges area of France. The unit markings can be seen on the rear of the 105mm Assault Tank M4A3. Note the trailer loaded with 105mm HE shells attached to the tank.

October 30, 1944 (Williams) (165). Cpl. Robert Meyers of Illinois and Sgt. John Nolan of Alabama are pouring it to Jerry with their 75mm assault gun. This gun is mounted on an M8 tank that is dug in. 2nd Battalion, 66th Armored Regiment, 2nd Armored Division.

The 2nd Battalion, 66th Armored Regiment was moved from Oidtweilerweg to the area of Ubach and Alsdorf at the end of October for rest and refitting. This 75mm Howitzer Motor Carriage M8 crew have erected a canopy over their vehicle.

October 14, 1944 (Petrony) (165). A Mark VI German tank knocked out by our TD units overturned and landed in a ditch.

A Panther Ausf.G from Pz.Abt.2105 of Panzer-Brigade 105. It was probably bulldozed off the road in the foreground, turning over in the process.

November 3, 1944 (Musae) (166). GIs check and refuel their medium tank near Nancy, France. 737th Tank Battalion.

This Medium Tank M4 of the 737th Tank Battalion is ready for action, although between November 1 and 7, the unit was providing indirect fire support. Each platoon fired an average of 250 rounds a day in support of the 35th Infantry Division.

November 7, 1944 (Herold) (167). Position of placing a 105mm howitzer in LVT. 9th US Army.

In Forgotten Archives 1, we used a photo from the same sequence that showed 57mm and 75mm guns being loaded into a DUKW. Here we see a 105mm Howitzer M3 being loaded into an LVT(A) 2. They were clearly training for a river crossing.

November 13, 1944 (Bradley) (166). Tank destroyer waits turn to go into action in the Moselle River sector.

No unit is given for this 76mm Gun Motor Carriage M10 named 'Cobra,' and there were several tank destroyer units in the area at this time. The vehicle has a lot of stowage attached, including bedrolls, tarps, and personal rucksacks.

November 24, 1944 (Lapine) (166).

Pz.Jg.Abt.61 of 11.Panzer-Division received twenty new Jagdpanzers in November 1944. On the 22nd, they destroyed 10 American tanks in Saint-Jean-Rohrbach, probably from the 6th Armored Division, where this vehicle was lost. Note the famous 'gespenster' (ghost) insignia of 11.Pz.Div. on the bow armor.

December 2, 1944 (McCroby) (163).

GIs look over a Medium Tank M4A3 (76) with extensive damage to the driver's position and running gear. There is a second knocked out tank further down the road.

December 2, 1944 (McCroby) (163).

The M4A3 (76) from the previous page, with one of the GIs checking the closely grouped holes made by armor-piercing rounds. Based upon other photos of this tank, we know it was from the 14th Armored Division, near Barr, France.

December 6, 1944. 75mm assault gun StuG.40 in Company C area of 295th Engineers during the siege of Wurselen, in the distance.

A Sturmgeschütz III with 13 kill rings painted on the barrel was destroyed sometime earlier, probably October 17 or 18, and belonged to Sturmgeschütz-Brigade 394. Würselen church is in the left background.

December 9, 1944. 295th Engineers photo of Panther at Busbach.

A Panther of Panzer-Brigade 105 at Büsbach. Although the date in the caption is December 9, it was knocked out on September 16 after an engagement with the 3rd Armored Division. We know that two Panthers from Pz.Abt.2105 were engaged at Büsbach on September 16, one belonging to the battalion adjutant.

December 15, 1944 (Spangle). A 9th Division bazooka man knocked out this German tank as it was rolling through the town of Mariaweiler. A dead Nazi lies in the gutter.

According to the AAR of the 60th Infantry Regiment for December 12, the Germans counterattacked with two self-propelled guns, and one was knocked out. The Germans saw the thrust into Mariaweiler as a direct threat to Düren and counterattacked to eject the 9th Infantry Division. The vehicle is a Jagdpanzer 38 from Pz.Jg.Kp.1147, 47.Volksgrenadier-Division, knocked out while supporting the counterattack by Volks-Gren.Rgt.115.

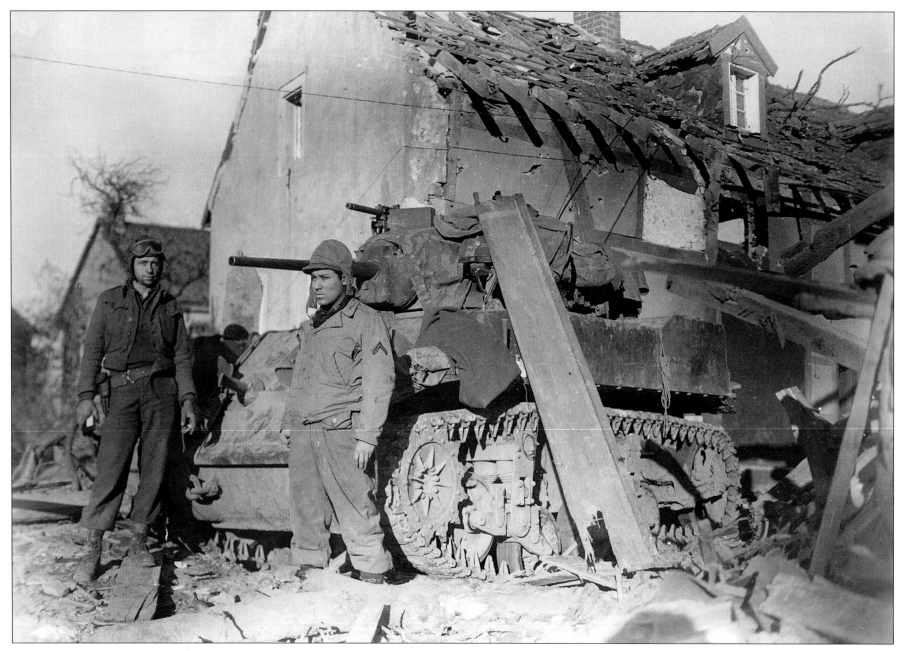

December 29, 1944. Light tank of 113th Cavalry attached to 295th Engineers for defense of Roer river.

GIs from 113th Cavalry Reconnaissance Squadron pose with their Light Tank M5A1 while supporting the 295th Engineers in Strass, Germany. Of interest here is the length of wood leaning against the tank to help disguise its profile, and the German 'Zeltbahn' on top of the tank.

December 29, 1944. M8 scout car of 113th Cavalry attached to the 295th Engineers for the defense of the Roer River.

Another vehicle from 113th Cavalry Reconnaissance Squadron supporting the 295th Engineers in Strass; this one a Light Armored Car M8. Strass is on the outskirts of the Hürtgen Forest, and the conditions in this photo are typical of the period.

December 5, 1944 (Colwell) (166). Two soldiers of the Victory Division inspect a German tank that was stopped by fire from a tank mounted cannon in Saarlautern, Germany. The tank, which was loaded with TNT and dynamite, failed to blow up and was halted 100 yards from its destination. 1st Battalion, 379th Infantry Regiment, 95th Infantry Division.

This burnt-out Pz.Kpfw.IV Ausf.J, from I./ Pz.Rgt.22, 21.Panzer-Division, was one of two destroyed while supporting a counterattack on a bridge in Saarlautern by Kampfgruppe Lier.

William Tomko of the 166th SPC took this photo. No date or location is given, but it looks to be France in the Autumn of 1944; at this time, Tomko covered the 90th Infantry Division. Here, three Sturmgeschütz III, with concrete over the front of the fighting compartment, have been blown up by their crews as all have the roofs missing.

December 5, 1944 (Williams) (167). Member of 9th Army armored unit checks his anti-freeze as winter approaches in Baesweiler, Germany. 14th Field Artillery Battalion, 2nd Armored Division.

A GI gets this Half-track Personnel Carrier M3A1 ready for the upcoming winter weather. The marking on the hood that indicates that antifreeze has been added to the vehicle already. Some vehicles had 'Prestone 44' as the marking instead. The chains on the wheels will improve traction in ice and snow.

December 6, 1944 (Anders) (166). A Sherman tank with a bulldozer blade grades area at the wrecked railroad station at Hemmersdorf, Germany, on the Saar River front. 712th Tank Battalion, 90th Infantry Division.

A Medium Bulldozer Tank M4 adorned with a framed photo of Hitler on the front. The 712th Tank Battalion was in action on either side of the Saar at this time, while the Service Company moved into Hemmersdorf on December 3.

December 6, 1944 (Anders) (166). The two large wheels mounted in front of this American tank in the Saar River sector in Germany are designed to clear a safe path for the tanks through enemy minefields. The large wheels which are comprised of steel discs are geared to the treads and will explode mines in the tank's path without damaging the tank. 712th Tank Battalion, 90th Infantry Division.

A Mine Exploder T1E3 (M1) of 712th Tank Battalion attached to the 90th Infantry Division moves down a road as they conduct operations on the German side of the Saar River in early December 1944. The unit was only in this area for a few weeks before being called to assist with the Ardennes Counteroffensive in Luxembourg.

December 10, 1944 (Ornitz) (166). German tank knocked out by US armor lies beneath a fallen tree in the wooded section of Domfessel, France.

A Panther Ausf.G completed by M.N.H. in July or early August 1944 from II./Pz-Lehr. Rgt.130, Panzer-Lehr-Division. This unit was in combat around Domfessel, although there were no reported losses of Panthers at this time.

December 10, 1944 (Sanderson) (167). The crew of a dug-in tank destroyer on alert for enemy activity in the 9th Army Sector of Germany, in the turret is T/5 L.C. Altman, of Reynolds, IN.; Pfc. Al Sehlmo, Atlantic City, N.J., observer, and Pvt. S.R. Haislip, Washington D.C., right. Co. C, 3rd Platoon, 638th Tank Battalion, 9th US Army.

The 638th Tank Destroyer Battalion was equipped with the 76mm Gun Motor Carriage M18 and attached to the 84th Infantry Division. At this time, they were in the Prummern area before moving to Frelenberg on December 12 and then to the Ardennes.

December 15, 1944 (Sanderson) (167). Ordnance men work on a captured German tank; it was captured near Gersonweiler, Germany.

This is the first clear image of this well known Tiger II that shows the tactical number '211'. The Tiger was from s.H.Pz.Abt.506 and captured by US ordnance men who freed the turret after it was hit by an American shell, before taking it for a joy ride. See Panzerwrecks 5 for more photos and information.

November 24, 1944 (Herold) (3264). Three Yanks pause in their Jeep to look over a wrecked German mobile gun. L to R: S/Sgt. Richard Infantino, Sgt. Arthur Stockhoff and Pvt. James Vitola. Sgt. Stockhoff is a Signal Corps photographer.

The 'mobile gun' is a Jagdpanzer 38. On February 5, 1945, the photographer, T/4 William Herold, was killed in action along with Sgt. Arthur Stockhoff, who is pictured sitting in the Jeep. According to their CO, they were killed while evacuating wounded soldiers from a bombed building.

January 1, 1945. Sherman tank with 76mm gun knocked out near Strass, 295th Engineers sector.

A Medium Tank M4A3 (76), probably from the 774th Tank Battalion, which moved to Strass in mid-December to support the 83rd Infantry Division. The tank seems to have suffered track damage from a mine, and the AAR for December mentions at least four tanks being disabled by mines early on. The 464th Ordnance Company has tagged it for inspection and removal.

FIELD MODIFICATIONS & TESTS
Cameramen Visit Ordnance Units

September 13, 1944 (Gedicks) (165). Member of tank crew shows flame thrower now mounted as part of a medium tank armament in place of a 0·30 cal MG.

The soldier holds an E4-5 flamethrower, installed in tanks of the 70th Tank Battalion in September 1944 to test their effectiveness.

November 7, 1944 (Guinn) (167). Close-up of the wasp, a new mechanical flame thrower mounted on the back of a half track at a chemical warfare testing ground somewhere in Holland. 9th US Army, Maastricht, Holland.

There was a delay in equipping US tanks with flamethrowers, so the Army experimented with a Wasp flamethrower on a halftrack. The weapon was impressive, but all agreed that a halftrack was far too vulnerable.

November 7, 1944 (Guinn) (167). Action shot of wasp, a new mechanical flame thrower mounted on the back of a half track at a chemical warfare testing ground somewhere in Holland. 9th US Army, Maastricht, Holland.

This photo shows the range the Wasp was able to project to, but as noted in the previous photo, the testers agreed a halftrack was too vulnerable to be the weapon platform.

97

▲ March 9, 1945 (Newell) (163). Front view of a T-34 multiple rocket launcher on an M4A3 Medium Tank.

'Cold Storage', a Rocket Launcher T34 (Calliope), was shown in Forgotten Archives 2. This image offers a good three-quarter view so that the whole tank can be seen. Note the two German helmets and M3 submachine gun hanging off the front.

▶ February 8, 1945 (Harding) (166). Rocket tanks in Luxembourg City. 501st Ordnance Battalion.

A great side view of a T-34 Calliope seen in Forgotten Archives 1, page 163. No unit is given, but the remains of whitewash and location of Luxembourg would most likely make this a 3rd Army tank. Note the cooking and eating supplies on the back and the attached wire for camouflage.

December 9, 1944 (Rosenmann) (165). Test firing of a 90mm Tank Destroyer of the 703rd against a German Panther.

Panther '214' of Pz.Rgt.24, 116.Panzer-Division was captured near Stolberg in early December. The 703rd Tank Battalion, attached to the 3rd Armored Division, conducted firing tests on it with 90mm guns. The results showed the 90mm was effective against the Panther's frontal armor.

September 17, 1944. A tank of the 743rd Tank Battalion used to carry a section of Bailey bridge near Gulpen, Holland.

Gulpen is west of Aachen. This Medium Tank M4A1, from the 743rd Tank Battalion, is carrying a section of Bailey bridge with a rudimentary lift attached by the 295th Engineer Combat Battalion. The devices on the headlamp guard are track jacks, used to remove end connectors and pull track ends together.

August 8, 1944 (Norbuth) (165). M5 light tank with Rhino attachment, 747th Tank Battalion, France.

A Light Tank M5A1, number 'D-2' from 'D' Company, 747th Tank Battalion, supporting the 29th Infantry Division. It was fitted with a 'Cullin' cutter device in July 1944.

August 8, 1944 (Norbuth) (165). M4 medium tank with prong attachment, which is used for making holes into high dirt banks into which explosives are placed for blasting. 747th Tank Battalion, France.

A Medium Tank M4, number '9' of an unknown company, shows off a different type of hedgerow cutter known as a 'salad fork.' This photograph has been seen before but not in such high quality.

August 8, 1944 (Norbuth) (165).

The driver of A-18, a Medium Tank M4 fitted with a 'Cullin' cutter device, drives towards the cameraman. Judging by the dirt on the cutter, the tank has probably demonstrated its capabilities.

C-16, 'Candy' from the 747th Tank Battalion, is fitted with a Calliope rocket system and is shown here being tested in Germany in the Fall of 1944. Notice the various control wires hanging down and the wet, muddy conditions.

'Candy', from the previous page, fires a salvo of rockets in front of an audience of spectators.

November 25, 1944 (Dougall) (166). Pfc. Ignacio Solis of El Paso TX attaches a rack to his Jeep which has many accessory features, Morhange, France.

A senior officer probably used this modified Jeep. The bumper markings are for the HQ of 17th Armored Group, XII Corps, 3rd Army.

December 26, 1944 (Shub) (165). An enemy motor pool containing self-propelled guns, halftracks and other types of vehicles destroyed by 30th Division near La Gleize, Belgium.

At least seven different Sd.Kfz.251s from Kampfgruppe Peiper can be seen in this photo, including a Sd.Kfz.251/21 variant. The location is the Pré de Froidecour orchard, south of La Gleize.

December 26, 1944 (Shub) (165). German self-propelled gun captured by the 30th Division near La Gleize, Belgium.

One of six Sd.Kfz.138/1 Ausf.M (Grille) of 13.(IG)/SS-Pz.Gren.Rgt.2, left in La Gleize by Kampfgruppe Peiper when elements of the 30th Infantry and 3rd Armored Divisions captured the town. The photo shows the interior of the fighting compartment with radio racks to good effect and the 'L' shaped supports for a tarp.

December 27, 1944 (Shub) (165). German AA tank knocked out by American forces in the La Gleize area of Belgium.

Before making his way to La Gleize, Shub photographed a knocked out Wirbelwind (based on a rebuilt Pz.Kpfw.IV Ausf.H chassis) from 10.(Fla)/SS-Pz.Rgt.1 in front of the Sanatorium St-Edouard in Stoumont. It was destroyed by 119th Infantry Regiment, 30th Infantry Division.

Flakpanzer IV 'Wirbelwind'
10.(Fla)/SS-Pz.Rgt.1, 1.SS-Panzer-Division
Stoumont, Belgium
December 27, 1944

▲ December 27, 1944 (Shub) (165). Front view of knocked out Nazi Mark V tank put out of action by American forces in the La Gleize area of Belgium.

A well-known Panther in La Gleize. This low shot shows Panther '221' from SS-Pz. Rgt.1. It looks as if both the mantlet and glacis plate have been penetrated. This Panther was one of the test series fitted with steel tyred wheels.

▶ December 27, 1944 (Ryan) (166). Soldier of the 26th Infantry Division inspects a blasted Nazi Tiger tank near Eschdorf, Luxembourg, 104th Regiment, 26th Infantry Division.

The 26th Infantry Division fought in Eschdorf between December 23 and 25. The Sturmgeschütz III is either from 5./Fhr.Gren.Btl. or StuG.Brig.911, attached to Fhr. Gren.Brig. as of December 1944 and incorporated after the Ardennes Offensive.

December 29, 1944. Photos taken of the 238th Combat Engineer Battalion.

Tiger '104' of s.SS-Pz.Abt.501 being inspected by General Dawley and his men in La Gleize. The tank was abandoned by its crew on December 23 after breaking down and was subsequently used for bazooka target practice by the 82nd Airborne Division.

December 30, 1944. (Gilbert) (166). A knocked-out German Panther tank that tried to break into Bastogne.

This is a Sturmgeschütz III, with two more in the background. These vehicles are most likely from Kampfgruppe Maucke of Pz.Abt.115, 15.Panzergrenadier-Division, that led an attack down the Champs-Hemroulle road near Rolley, Belgium, against the 101st Airborne Division on Christmas day.

December 30, 1944. (Harding) (166). A view of a German armored car that had been knocked out by a bazooka fire near Lellig, Luxembourg. It had a mortar mounted in it.

Front and back of a frozen Leichter Panzerspähwagen (2cm) (Sd.Kfz.222) Ausf.B knocked out near Lellig on the German-Luxembourg border, west of Trier. There were no engagements here during the Battle of the Bulge, so the vehicle was probably lost in September. The armament was not a mortar, but a 2cm gun, here without its barrel. Note the umbrella insignia on the turret. AMC

January 2, 1945 (Kitzerow) (165). S/Sgt. Gene Taylor, Kenton Ohio, and Pvt. Charles Lands, Athens Tenn., talk things over between fire missions on the Stavelot, Belgium front. 987th Field Artillery Battalion, Battery A, attached to 30th Infantry Division.

With the caption saying this is Battery A, there must be a word beginning with 'A' in front of 'Warrior' painted on the side. The 987th Armored Field Artillery Battalion was equipped with the 155mm Gun Motor Carriage M12, seen here. Both soldiers seem relaxed, an indication of being behind the frontline and having the Germans on the run.

January 3, 1945 (Petrony) (165). 82nd Airborne Division infantrymen ride into Trou-de-Bra, Belgium on tanks. They came in to take over the town, which had previously been softened up by the tanks of the 3rd Armored Division. 2nd Battalion, 32nd Armored Regiment, 3rd Armored Division.

This Assault Tank M4A3E2 (75) is carrying paratroopers from the 82nd Airborne Division into Trou de Bra to prepare to take the next town. Petrony photographed 105mm assault guns firing outside the village and must have returned as additional units were moving in.

January 3, 1945 (Lapine) (166). Enemy armored vehicles knocked out by the 6th Armored Division when the Nazis tried to take the town of Neffe, Belgium.

This snow-covered scene shows two Panthers from Pz.Rgt.130, Panzer-Lehr-Division, on the Rue de Clervaux in Neffe. The lead tank is numbered '533,' and both were knocked out by the 6th Armored Division.

January 10, 1945 (Valentine) (163). Cpl. Larry Hervier, Tupper Lake, NY, lowers himself into the driver's hatch of his medium tank that has just been whitewashed so it will blend with the snow-covered landscape. 753rd Tank Battalion, 36th Infantry Division.

After a few days of rest and refitting, the 753rd would be back in action around Hagenau, France. The tank is a Medium Tank M4 (75).

The 238th Engineer Combat Battalion knocked out five Panthers from 2.SS-Panzer-Division in a snowy field outside of Grandmenil on December 25, 1944. All were knocked out by an extensive minefield planted by the 238th.

Another of the 2.SS Panthers in the minefield. It looks as if the crew has attempted to repair their tank as the jack is in position on the rear tow pintle.

Outside La Gleize, the crew of a 155mm Gun Motor Carriage M12 from 987th Field Artillery Battalion await their next fire mission. The vehicle is covered with camouflage netting over large hoops.

105 mm Howitzer Motor Carriage M7s and crews from the 400th Field Artillery Battalion share a light moment between fire missions and the bitterly cold weather outside La Gleize. The M7 nearest the camera is named 'Bat Outta Hell.'

125

January 8, 1945 (Runyan) (165). Tanks of a British tank convoy pull trucks up an icy hill until they, in turn, skid on slick roads near Leignon, Belgium. 51st Highland Division.

It is easy to forget that the British were involved in the Ardennes. The '52' on this Medium Tank M4A2 denotes that it is from 1st Battalion, Coldstream Guards, 5th Guards Armored Brigade, Guards Armored Division; part of the British XXX Corps assisting the Americans in the northern sector of the Bulge.

January 8, 1945 (Runyan) (165). Bren gun carriers of a British convoy avoid slick roads in the Leignon area by cutting across country. 51st Highland Division.

The next photo in Runyan's series was of a column of Universal Carriers taking the cross-country route. The lead vehicle carries the name 'Bayswater.'

January 9, 1945 (Jones) (162). Sgt. Howard Gale of NH, with his umbrella, walks by an M-7 tank of the 3rd Army in Morhet, Belgium.

The censor didn't do the best job. We can see that this 105 mm Howitzer Motor Carriage M7 named 'Carmela' is from 'C' Company, 492nd Field Artillery Battalion, 11th Armored Division. Note the neatly stacked spent shell casings.

January 10, 1945 (Slevin) (167). 75mm armor-piercing shell entered center turret, passed through the gun carriage, and blew out the opposite side of this German tank near Chenogne, Belgium.

Two Panzer IV/70(A)s from Führer-Begleit-Brigade knocked out by the 11th Armored Division between December 28 and 30. Based on other photos, we know the nearest vehicle had the tactical number '111'.

January 10, 1945 (Slevin) (167). German tank with two other knocked out tanks in Chenogne, Belgium.

Looking back at the Panzer IV/70(A)s on the previous page. The vehicle in the foreground (believed to be tactical number '114') was hit in the rear plate, which has destroyed the running gear and popped the hull armor open. **AMC**

January 10, 1945 (Slevin) (167). German tank sits abandoned in a field near Chenogne, Belgium.

A fourth Panzer IV/70(A), with no visible damage, and still with foliage attached. Although difficult to see here, the tank has four steel-tired wheels at the front. **AMC**

January 14, 1945 (Mastrosimone) (3264). To provide cheap and effective camouflage paint for vehicles in snow, men of a cavalry recon unit mix lime to make whitewash for M-8 Armored Car. Co. F, Recon Troop, 4th Infantry Division.

Two photos showing a recon unit of the 4th Infantry Division mixing and applying a rudimentary whitewash to their M8 Light Armored Cars. Here, soldiers crush the lime and mix it with water to form a solution that can be applied by brush.

January 14, 1945 (Mastrosimone) (3264). Using whitewash just mixed, men of 4th Infantry Division Reconnaissance unit paint their M-8 Armored Car with the solution. Co. F, Recon Troop, 4th Infantry Division.

With the whitewash mixed, the troops begin to apply it to their armored cars. It is interesting that the caption states 'F' Company, whereas the vehicle in the photo has markings of 'C' Company.

January 15, 1945. (Signal Corps photo supplied to press). Snow and ice give the average motorist plenty of trouble, but even tanks occasionally come to grief in skiddy weather. First Army men tie a tow chain to a US tank, which slid off the slippery road somewhere on the Belgian front.

This Medium Tank M4A3 (75) has slipped off the road and into a ditch. Maintenance men attach a tow cable from an armored recovery vehicle to extract it. 'First Army' does not help identify the unit. **AMC**

January 1945 (166).

A Panzer IV/70(V) with a scar from a near miss on the side of the fighting compartment and damaged return roller. The latter probably happened when it was pushed off the road. **AMC**

January 17, 1945 (Coughlin) (166). Part of Combat Command B, 10th Armored Division, this M-8 reconnaissance car has just returned to Metz from the Belgian front in the Bastogne sector.

This is an Armored Utility Car M20 with the remains of a scruffy coat of whitewash. The 10th Armored Division was hit hard in the early days of the Ardennes Offensive and was moved to France to rest and refit.

January 22, 1945 (Anders) (166). US Sherman tank hit at Longvilly, Belgium, by German bazooka fire, ordnance tank retriever prepares to haul it out. 90th Infantry Division, 128th Ordnance Battalion.

The markings on the back of this whitewashed Medium Tank M4 (75) show that it was from the 68th Tank Battalion, 6th Armored Division. The tank's gun has left a mark on the wall of the house as it was driven, or more likely pulled by the recovery vehicle. The tracks have been removed to make it easier to recover.

January 2, 1945 (Carolan) (165). Crew members of a 7th Armored Division tank check their Sherman tank near Les Baty Belgium. 17th Tank Battalion, 7th Armored Division.

An Assault Gun M4 (105) from HQ Company, 17th Tank Battalion. According to the January 2 after-action report, the unit was taken off the one hour alert that morning and devoted the rest of the day to maintenance. The vehicle has evergreen branches attached for extra camouflage.

January 23, 1945 (Mallinder) (166). Men of Company D, 42nd Tank Battalion, stand around a fire near their tanks, awaiting orders to move on. This is in the town of Steinbach, Belgium.

The 'Battle of the Bulge' was as good as over by this time, and these two M4A3 (75)s have missed out on a coat of whitewash, making them stand out against the snow. The crews make the most of the fire they have made.

There is no caption for this photo as it was scanned from a negative taken by Lt. Joe Zinni of the 166th Signal Photo Co. The date is January 1945, and the location is Esch Sur-la-Sûre in Luxembourg. These M10s are from the 818th Tank Destroyer Battalion, attached to the 26th Infantry Division, and are being whitewashed. The AAR noted that it had to be reapplied regularly as it quickly wore off. Note the hedgerow cutters on both M10s.

Another of Zinni's photos, this showing an ex-Italian SPA TL37 artillery tractor, its only German addition being a 'Notek' headlamp. Zinni shot this during January 1945 in the area of Tarchamps and Watrange, Luxembourg.

February 3, 1945 (Makarewicz) (165). This American M-8 recon car was captured by the Germans and later knocked out by American artillery in the town of Honsfeld, Belgium.

A Light Armored Car M8 sits knocked out in Honsfeld, which had been recaptured by the 18th Infantry Regiment a few days earlier on January 30. The M8 is missing the two wheels on this side and probably on the other side too. While the caption indicates it was used by the Germans, the only visible markings are American. AMC

February 28, 1945 (Newhouse) (166). German armored halftrack and 88mm gun put out of action by Allied bombers on the 6th Armored Division front near Dasburg, Germany.

This wreckage was pushed off the road onto this unfortunate building. On the left is a Sd.Kfz.251/3, next to it a Steyr 1500. Further down is an overturned French artillery tractor and an 8·8cm Pak 43. A number of units retreated over the Our River making an ID impossible.

11TH ARMORED DIVISION
From the Ardennes to Germany with the Thunderbolt Division

January 10, 1945 (Slevin) (166). Pfc. Davis of Texas paints a 76mm gun with whitewash to camouflage it while T/4 William Aberer of Hoboken puts finishing touches. Co. B, 41st Tank Battalion, 11th Armored Division, Bercheux.

Forgotten Archives 2 showed this tank, a Medium Tank M4A3 (76), and crew painting their helmets. The 41st Tank Battalion moved to Bercheux on January 3 for rest and refitting.

January 16, 1945 (166). M4A3 Sherman tank of the 42nd Tank Battalion rolls out of Compiegne, en route to Houffalize, Belgium. A muzzle brake is mounted on the tank gun. Company B.

A Medium Tank M4A3 (76) HVSS heads out from Compiègne, Belgium. It is probably a replacement and has no whitewash.

January 17, 1945 (McDonald) (166). A knocked-out German tank lies in a shell hole in Noville, Belgium. It was knocked out by elements of the 11th Armored Division.

A Sturmgeschütz III, probably from 2.Panzer-Division, knocked out and pushed into a bomb crater opposite the church in Noville. This view shows the details of the roof and engine deck to good effect.

145

Men from the 11th Armored Division move past two abandoned Panzer IV/70(V)s near Hoscheid. Both have been 'short-tracked' and probably towed under the trees for repair, but were subsequently destroyed. The location, date and US unit all point to the vehicles belonging to III.(Pz.)/Führer-Grenadier-Brigade, whose 12 Kompanie was allocated eleven of these vehicles.

Being taken by an 11th Armored Division photographer, this wrecked Tiger II is probably from s.Pz.Abt.506. An explosion has thrown the turret (an initial version with rounded front) to the side of the tank and blown out one of the hull sides.

147

A Light Tank M5A1 of the 41st Cavalry Reconnaissance Squadron, 11th Armored Division named 'Bernice' sits on watch outside a German bunker on the Siegfried Line near Lutzkampen, Germany. After-action reports state that the 41st had a command post in an abandoned bunker on February 14, 1945, after the 11th Armored cleared the area.

148

A Light Armored Car M8 of 'B' Troop, 41st Cavalry Reconnaissance Squadron with four German POWs being brought in for processing. The M8 has remnants of whitewash, an air recognition panel, ammo boxes, and a case of K9 rations. The date is mid-February 1945 on the Luxembourg-Germany border.

A Light Tank M5A1 from the 11th Armored Division makes its way across the Rhine River, with another waiting on the river bank. No date is provided, but given the 11th's route and history, it is around mid-March 1945.

7TH ARMY PART 1
Operation Nordwind

January 31, 1945 (Leibowitz) (163). Tanks of the 749th Tank Battalion in Weisviller, France, held in readiness for direct support of the infantry, which at present controls the ground around the town.

At this time, the 749th Tank Battalion was in XV Corps reserve, ready to move at 6 hours notice. The AAR report for the 749th noted that they had 43 medium and 17 light tanks operational at the end of the month. Both M4s here are whitewashed and have sandbags on the front.

February 7, 1945 (Miller) (163). Sherman tank mounting new 76mm gun knocked out by German tank fire. Co. A, 25th Tank Battalion, 14th Armored Division. Oberfhoffen area, France.

This Medium Tank M4A3 (76) was hit by anti-tank rounds which started a fire that consumed the vehicle. The 14th Armored Division was in close-combat with 275. Volksgrenadier-Division and 10.SS-Panzer-Division in Oberhoffen.

Medium Tank M4A3 (76)
25th Tank Battalion, 14th Armored Division
Oberhoffen, France
February 7, 1945

February 1, 1945 (Newell) (163). An ordnance party examines the remains of a German Mark V Panther tank on a street in a small French village. Hit at right front, the shell penetrated the right side above the bogies. 134th Ordnance Battalion, 12th Armored Division, Kilstett, France.

The spare tracks on the turret of this Panther Ausf.G and the style of the hooks suggest that it is a survivor of I./SS-Pz.Rgt.10 from the Arnhem fighting. These were subsequently taken over by II./SS-Pz.Rgt.10 before being knocked out around January 18, 1945, on the outskirts of Kilstett, France, during Operation Nordwind.

February 1, 1945 (Newell) (163). Two German Panther tanks stand in a field outside of a small French town where they were destroyed by anti-tank fire. One was destroyed by a ricochet that hit the lower side of the gun shield and went down into the turret compartment, igniting the ammunition. 134th Ordnance Battalion, 12th Armored Division.

Two more Panthers from II./SS-Pz.Rgt.10 knocked out while attacking Kilstett around January 18, 1945. The tank in the foreground was initially issued to 5./SS-Pz.Rgt.10 and still has the black '534' tactical number on the turret side despite having suffered a catastrophic explosion that has blown the turret roof off. It has the relatively rare 'disc' pattern overlay on the factory-applied camouflage scheme.

February 4, 1945 (Newell) (163). A platoon of M4A3 medium tanks stand covering the edge of the forest 300 yards ahead while infantry dig positions. Allied forces attacked south of Colmar, and the nearest tank mounts a new 76mm gun with new muzzle brake and new type of suspension. Co. B, 714th Tank Battalion, CCB, 12th Armored Division. Colmar area, France.

A platoon of 12th Armored Division tanks: a Medium Tank M4A3 (76) HVSS, three Medium Tanks M4A3 (76), and another Medium Tank M4A3 (76) HVSS with a coat of whitewash on each provide cover for the attached armored infantry.

February 5, 1945 (Newell) (163). Crew poses with the first tank to enter Rouffach, France. The town was the junction for north and south Allied forces cutting off the Vosges pocket for the Germans. 12th Armored Division.

This Light Tank M5A1 survived the beating the 12th Armored Division took at Herrlisheim and was able to take part in closing the Colmar pocket.

▲ February 8, 1945 (Valentine) (163). Tank dozer tries to push this knocked out American medium tank off the road and leave it clear for military traffic. The tank was knocked out more than two weeks ago when the battle was taking place. Herrlisheim, France.

A Bulldozer M1A1 mounted on a Medium Tank M4A1 pushing a wrecked Medium Tank M4A3 (75) from the 12th Armored Division, who suffered catastrophic losses in and around Herrlisheim. This tank has a rudimentary assembly of sandbags on the side, which had no effect on the German anti-tank round penetrating the side.

▶ February 9, 1945 (Stubenrauch) (163). Knocked out German vehicle in Hettenschlag, France.

A great close up of a Flakpanzer IV 'Wirbelwind' (on a rebuilt Pz.Kpfw.IV late Ausf.G or early Ausf.H) from s.H.Pz.Jg.Abt.654, captured by troops of the 75th Infantry Division. It has a rough and worn coat of whitewash, and three of the four muzzle brakes are missing.

February 10, 1945 (Newell) (163). A light and medium tank lay in a flooded ditch on the outskirts of a French town after a battle. 43rd Tank Battalion, 12th Armored Division, Herrlisheim, France.

In a roadside ditch outside Herrlisheim, the wreckage of an Assault Gun M4A3 (105) and Light Tank M5A1. Both tanks have suffered a catastrophic explosion that blew the turrets off. The M5A1's roof has been stoved inwards, possibly indicating an artillery strike.

February 13, 1945 (Weintraub) (163). An American T-2 tank retriever is shown recovering a German light tank which Americans once shot up. Now it will be used for target practice. 12th Armored Division, Munster area, France.

The tank retriever is a Tank Recovery Vehicle M32. The 'light tank' is a Sturmgeschütz IV, which has been demolished by the crew setting charges in the engine and fighting compartments.

February 13, 1945 (Bell) (163). Knocked out American tank and German self-propelled gun sit side by side in a street of Oberhoffen. Note hit on German self-propelled gun.

The Medium Tank M4 is probably from the 14th Armored Division who fought against 257.Volksgrenadier-Division and 10.SS-Panzer-Division in Oberhoffen, although 10.SS.Pz.Div. no longer had Stugs at this point. The Sturmgeschütz was knocked out by a close grouping of shots into the bow.

February 15, 1945 (Valentine) (163). This American medium tank knocked out by German bazooka fire, stands in front of a shell wrecked building in Herrlisheim, France.

One of many 12th Armored Division tanks lost in and around Herrlisheim. An after-action report written by a graves registration unit noted that almost all the destroyed tanks in Herrlisheim were accounted for by Panzerfausts and bazookas, while those in the fields around the town were from high-velocity anti-tank guns.

This Medium Tank M4A3 (76) from 'A' Company, 43rd Tank Battalion, was one of many lost in Herrlisheim and appears to have been hit in the side several times. Subsequently, the glacis plate was cut out, presumably to up-armor another tank. After the battle, the 12th Armored Division plotted the knocked out tanks on a map.

March 12, 1945 (Newell) (163). Test firing. M4 tank used as a target to test sandbag and armor plate reinforcement on tanks. Here is the opposite side of the tank where the shell came through three layers of armor. 134th Ordnance Battalion, 12th Armored Division, Faulquemont, France.

A Medium Tank M4A3 (75)W from 43rd Tank Battalion probably removed from the Herrlisheim battlefield. The firing tests were carried out on the opposite side of the tank, and we see here two exit holes and what is best described as a deformation of the armor plate.

T/4 WARREN ROTHENBERGER

166th Signal Photo Company

Technician 4th Grade Warren Rothenberger was with the 166th Signal Photographic Company for the entirety of the war in Europe, photographing the advance of the 90th and 26th Infantry Divisions. He received a Bronze Star for his photographic actions under fire at a bridge over the Moselle River near the villages of Catternon and Malling, France. I want to thank his daughters Lisa and Jann McAleer and their husbands, Jim and John, for their use of Mr. Rothenberger's photos.

November 2, 1944 (Rothenberger) (166). Soldiers fend off chill with small fire they have built in front of their Sherman tank somewhere in France. 712th Tank Battalion, 90th Infantry Division, Urcourt, France.

The 712th Tank Battalion was in Joudreville for rest and refitting before moving towards Sentzich a week later to cross the Moselle River. It is interesting to note that each man sports different headgear.

November 5, 1944 (Rothenberger) (166). Agents of Division CIC team check halftrack self-propelled gun knocked out of action near Mairy, France. Vehicles were used for bazooka training. 90th Infantry Division.

Not one, not two, but three Sd.Kfz.251/21s and a Sd.Kfz.251/9, all from Panzer-Brigade 106, sit in a collection area. The vehicle in the foreground is a standard infantry carrier. Rothenberger also photographed a GI on the Sd.Kfz.251/9's engine deck.

November 9, 1944 (Rothenberger) (166). Tank crew climbs aboard their tank prior to moving up on the Moselle River front. 712th Tank Battalion. Sentizch, Germany.

This is probably a staged photograph of a Medium Tank M4 and crew. The unit did not cross until November 12, so Rothenberger probably asked for an 'action' shot. The location is Sentzich in France.

November 17, 1944 (Rothenberger) (166).

According to the AAR of the 712th Tank Battalion, 'C' Company had a tank damaged by a bazooka, but it was not knocked out and returned to action. The tank is a Medium Tank M4A3 (76).

November 26, 1944 (Rothenberger) (166). Self-propelled 155mm gun on M12 firing towards Siegfried Line defense outside German village. 558th Field Artillery Battalion, 10th Armored Division.

'Charley's Champion,' a 155mm Gun Motor Carriage M12, lobs shells onto German defenses at the border, with two more M12s in the background. The vehicle has a camouflage pattern applied on its side.

170

This is probably the 3-Inch GMC M10 from 'B' Company, 773rd Tank Destroyer Battalion seen in the background of the next page, its field modified cover over the turret being the same. To the left is a captured British truck modified by the Germans, and next to this a limber from a German gun.

171

▲ December 15, 1944 (Rothenberger) (166). Men of the 773rd Tank Destroyer Battalion, attached to the 90th Infantry Division, load ammo for their 3-inch guns in Wallerfangen, Germany.

Two photos showing 3-inch Gun Motor Carriage M10s and their crews from 'B' Company, 773rd Tank Destroyer Battalion. This crew is loading 3-inch shells from crates. Note the significant amount of crew stowage around the turret.

▶ December 15, 1944 (Rothenberger) (166). Soldiers of the 773rd Tank Destroyer Battalion, attached to the 90th Infantry Division, answer mail call in Wallerfangen, Germany.

Taking a break from loading ammunition, the crews are given their mail. Note the small details of soldiers in the field: the lack of bootlaces on the left and the twin headgear combo of the guy on the ammunition boxes.

January 19, 1945 (Rothenberger) (166). Men of the 90th Infantry Division brush the snow from their Sherman tank after heavy snow outside of Doncols, Luxembourg. 712th Tank Battalion.

A front view of this Medium Tank M4 was shown in Forgotten Archives 1. Here, a different cameraman from the same team, Rothenberger, captures the rear.

(Rothenberger) (166).

Warren Rothenberger was attached to the 26th Infantry after the Bulge, and he noted this location as being St Barbara, Germany, which is near Wallerfangen, see the fallen road sign. The Medium Tank M4 undergoing a track repair probably belongs to the 778th Tank Battalion, attached to the 26th.

175

A Light Tank M5A1 stands guard on a street corner in Ottweiler, Germany, recently taken by the 26th Infantry Division. Rothenberger did not provide a unit ID for this photo, but it is probably from its attached tank battalion, the 778th Tank Battalion, or a cavalry unit, based on the tank commander's patch.

T/4 Warren Rothenberger

A serious card game for tankers of 'B' Company, 778th Tank Battalion, attached to the 26th Infantry Division, as the war winds down. Quite the assembly of tanks too, Left background: Assault Tank M4A3E2 upgraded with a 76mm gun. Foreground: M4A3 (75) W. Right background: Assault Tank M4A3E2 upgraded with a 76mm gun.

177

May 7, 1945 (Rothenberger) (166).

Elements of 11.Panzer-Division and Pz.Jg.Abt.553 surrendered to the 26th Infantry Division at Schwarzbach, and Rothenberger captured most of it. Here are three Jagdpanzer 38s, with a fourth on the right of the photo. The vehicle covered in foliage is a Befehlswagen.

May 7, 1945 (Rothenberger) (166).

A wider view of the Jagdpanzers, and we can see that a GI has painted 'USA' onto one. Martin Block details the short history of Pz.Jg.Abt.553: "Pz.-Jagd-Abt. 553 was an ad hoc unit formed in mid-April 1945 on the Milowitz training area using the Stab of Pz.Jäger-Abt.553 and two Jagdpanzer 38 companies originally intended for other infantry divisions. The unit left Milowitz by train during the night of 24./25.4.1945 intended for the Western Front but never made it there."

May 7, 1945 (Rothenberger) (166).

Rothenberger has moved down the hill for another shot and we can see the top of the 'Swastika' on the side of one of the Jagdpanzers. One of the crew chats with a local citizen.

May 7, 1945 (Rothenberger) (166).

One of the camouflaged Jagdpanzers makes its way up a hill in Schwarzbach, through the anti-tank barrier made of logs and rubble.

May 7, 1945 (Rothenberger) (166).

An excellent rear shot of one of the Jagdpanzer 38s, showing the insignia of Pz.Jg. Abt.553: a jousting knight on a Jagdpanzer. A couple of other points are notable; the wooden stowage bin added to the engine access hatch behind the commander, a common addition, and the two 'Jerrycans' in place of spare tracks.

February 23, 1945 (Massenge) (165). A First US Army tank destroyer fires at a German observation post across the Ruhr river near the town of Nideggen, Germany. Co. B, 899th Tank Destroyer Battalion, 60th Regiment, 9th Infantry Division.

At this time, the 899th Tank Destroyer Battalion was transitioning from the 3-Inch GMC M10 to the 90mm GMC M36. On February 23, 'B' Company fired 220 rounds of 3-inch ammunition into enemy bunkers and strongpoints from positions in Bergstein.

Ettelbruck.

The wrecked Panther Ausf.G on this and the next page are of tank '401' from Pz.Rgt.15, 11.Panzer-Division. Information with the photos states that they were lost in Ettelbruck near Bastogne. The 11.Pz.Div. was not engaged in the Ardennes action, and so this is an error in the caption.

Ettelbruck.

The front of tank '401', showing the turret has blown off. As noted, the 11.Pz.Div. was not involved in the Ardennes, but the style of numbers on this and the next page indicate that they are from this unit. The 315th Engineers served with the 90th Infantry Division, who fought 11.Pz.Div. near the Eifel region later in 1945.

Ettelbruck.

A few hundred yards away was '415', again from Pz.Rgt.15. The 11.Panzer-Division was the only unit with all-black tactical numbers on the western front. It appears that the Panther has backed itself up onto a tree and got stuck.

▲ March 23, 1945 (Nicholson) (167). Standing in front of a German Mark IV tank they knocked out near Titz, Germany.

This Pz.Kpfw.IV was likely from Pz.Rgt.15, 11.Panzer-Division. It was knocked out by Pfcs Melvin Ayres and Daniel Mixon of 115th Infantry Regiment, 29th Infantry Division. The bazooka round disabled the tank, and the crew were killed by a grenade down the hatch according to the after-action report.

▶ February 28, 1945 (Moran) (165). German Mark IV tank captured in Morschenich, Germany, during a surprise attack by 104th Infantry Division, 413th Infantry Regiment.

This Pz.Bef.Wg.IV Ausf.G was captured in Morschenich by the 413th Infantry Regiment, during their attack over the Roer River. It is probably from II./Pz.Rgt.15, and appears to be one of those inherited from 273.Res.Pz.Div. in May.

March 5, 1945 (Himes) (165). Tanks and infantrymen of the First U.S Army enter Cologne, Germany.

An Assault Tank M4A3E2 (75) re-armed with a 76mm gun of 'F' Company, 2nd Battalion, 32nd Armored Regiment, 3rd Armored Division. It stands in an overwatch position next to a railway overpass on Venloer Straße, on the outskirts of Cologne, Germany, on March 5, 1945. **AMC**

March 6, 1945 (Himes) (165). Nazi crew abandons German Mark V tank as M-26 tank of the First US Army scores a direct hit at 100 yards range in Cologne, Germany. (US tank not visible).

*A rare photo indeed. According to the caption, this is one of three photos showing the famous duel between a Pershing and Panther tank, the latter from 2./Pz.Abt.2106, Panzer-Brigade 106. The other well-known photo shows the Panther in flames after being hit by the Pershing. This photo appears to show the first hit, and the crew can be seen scrambling from the tank's hatches. **AMC***

March 7, 1945 (Dehart) (165). Lt. E. W. Gregson, of the 9th Armored Division, 1st US Army, looks over a knocked-out German 75mm self-propelled high-velocity tank. Lt. Gregson is from Indianapolis, Ind. Co. C, 19th Tank Bn., 9th Armd. Div., Germany.

A Sturmgeschütz III Ausf.G, on the side of a road in Germany. A US armor-piercing shot has embedded itself in the bow armor and dislodged one of the 'Schürzen.' One of the other tank battalions of the 9th Armored, the 14th, was taking the Ludendorff Bridge at Remagen on March 7, so this photo was probably taken in the area. Among the defending units were 89.Inf.Div., who reported 4 StuG III on February 28, so it probably belonged to Jagdpz.Kp.1189. **AMC**

March 11, 1945 (Calvano) (167). German prisoners are searched in front of their tank by men of the 8th Armored Division in Rheinberg, Germany.

A staged photo, taken in Winterswick on the southern outskirts of Rheinberg. The Sturmgeschütz III was knocked out by 2nd Lt. Wesley S. Buller, CO of 1st Platoon, 'B' Company, 36th Tank Battalion, 8th Armored Division. Two Sturmgeschütz units were in the area: 7./Pz.Rgt.16 of 116.Panzer-Division and Fallschirm-Stu.Gesch.Brig.12.

March 25, 1945 (Boland) (166). This is one of the 3rd US Army halftracks knocked out by enemy anti-tank guns between Oppan and Mannheim, Germany. 94th Infantry Division.

Photographer Boland probably means Oppau, which is across the river from Mannheim. This halftrack, an M3A1, belongs to 'A' Company of a 94th Infantry Division unit. It looks as if the anti-tank hit has set off the ammunition for the towed 57mm Gun M1, as spent ammunition covers the road.

March 20, 1945 (Elliott) (165). Looking at a knocked-out German tank destroyer are (left to right), 1st Lt Herbert Stackhouse, Dillion SC, and Pfc John Young, Winston Salem, NC, both with 39th Infantry Regiment, 9th Division, 1st US Army near Windhagen, Germany, near the Autobahn.

A Jagdpanther of s.Pz.Jg.Abt.654 destroyed outside Windhagen, Germany. 'C' Company of the 746th Tank Battalion with infantry from the 39th Infantry Regiment were counterattacked in the early morning of March 18 at the 'spiderweb' road net in Windhagen. The Germans attacked with five Jagdpanthers and knocked out a few American tanks, including an Assault Tank M4A3E2. However, two men from another crew were able to get back into the Jumbo and knock out one of the two Jagdpanthers. This is one of them. **AMC**

99th Infantry Division. March 1945.

The 393rd Infantry Regiment knocked out this Panther Ausf.G with a bazooka outside of Rothekruz, Germany. The tank, tactical number '516', is from II./Pz-Lehr. Rgt.130 and a survivor of the Ardennes Offensive.

February 25, 1945 (Nicholson) (167). 9th US Army tank returning from a recon tour on the outskirts of Stetternich, Germany.

No unit is given, but this Medium Tank M4A1 (75) is most likely from the 747th Tank Battalion, which was attached to the 29th Infantry Division at this time. A 3-Inch Gun Motor Carriage M10 is in the background.

April 21, 1945 (Lindgren) (168). A tank from the 8th Armored Division takes up position toward the burning town of Blankenburg, Germany.

A Medium Tank M4A3 76mm waits for the dust to settle before advancing into town. CCB of the 8th Armored Division, which included tanks from the 36th Tank Battalion, took the town after an aerial bombardment and negotiation with town officials.

April 11, 1945 (Boll) (168). Armor passing resting infantrymen in newly captured Braunschweig, taken by 30th Infantry Division.

The town is Ochsendorf, east of Braunschweig, and the infantry are from the 117th Infantry Regiment, 30th Infantry Division. The sandbagged Medium Tank M4A3 (75)W is probably from the 743rd Tank Battalion, who were attached to the 30th Infantry Division. The author's grandfather was a BAR gunner in the 119th Infantry Regiment, so this photo holds particular relevance.

V CORPS

From Col. Stanhope Mason, Chief of Staff, V Corps

October 9, 1944 (Franklin) (165). Vehicles belonging to an infantry unit move to Alsdorf, Germany, pass two knocked out US tanks.

These M4 Medium Tanks are from the 2nd Armored Division or 743rd Tank Battalion; both fought against Sturmgeschütz-Brigade 1012 around Aachen at this time. Both tanks have a penetration of the hull side and have burnt out.

November 15, 1944 (Gedicks) (165). Their flanks protected by a tank, 1st Division infantrymen advance through a German town hugging the wall on the right for protection from small arms fire. 1st Division, 26th Infantry Regiment, Zweifall, Germany.

'Charging' a Medium Tank M4 from 'C' Company, 745th Tank Battalion, provides cover for a squad of GIs from the 'Big Red One' in Zweifall.

December 4, 1944 (Crampton) (165). Sgt. Joseph Verhagen of Kaukauna, Wisconsin, observes the effect of fire from his tank gun on enemy positions in Hürtgen, Germany. 709th Tank Battalion, 8th Infantry Division.

This Medium Tank M4 is named' Blood & Guts' and was probably numbered 'B6' or 'B8'. A stowage rack has been welded to the rear of the turret and filled with much of the crew's stowage. The commander clearly is not observing the fall of his tank's shots as he is facing in the opposite direction!

December 4, 1944 (Crampton) (165). M4 tank firing on Nazi positions inside Hürtgen, Germany. 709th Tank Battalion, 8th Infantry Division.

No exact location is given but this Assault Gun M4 (105) could be one of two that fired over 100 rounds of 105mm at a church in Schmidt used as an observation post. In total, the 709th's assault gun platoon fired over 400 rounds in early December, in support of the 8th Infantry Division.

March 8, 1945 (Poinsett) (165). A Jeep pulls up alongside a Nazi vehicle in the town of Altenahr, which was entered on the evening of March 7, 1945, by 2nd Rangers and 38th Cavalry Reconnaissance Squadron.

A Jagdpanzer 38 destroyed after engaging light tanks of the 38th Cavalry Reconnaissance Squadron and GIs of the 2nd Ranger Battalion. The AAR of the 38th devotes two pages to actions in Altenahr, in which the advancing Americans caught the retreating Germans by surprise.

March 8, 1945 (Poinsett) (165). Nazi tank destroyed outside Altenahr taken by 38th Cavalry Reconnaissance Squadron and elements of the 2nd Ranger Battalion.

As the Jagdpanzer 38 was blocking the road, it was towed or pushed out of the way. The 20mm side armor, with ammunition stowed behind it, was prone to shattering when hit, leaving the 60mm thick front in situ. The only Jagdpanzer 38 equipped unit in the area was Jagdpz.Kp.1277 of 277.Volksgrenadier-Division.

March 13, 1945 (Benetsky) (165). Pfc. Royce A. Vick of Pittsburg PA, examines a decoy tank left behind by the Nazis after their swift retreat to the Rhine in Rodert, Germany. This tank consisted of a Mark IV tank chassis and the sides and turret made of wood. Believed to have been towed out into a field by the Germans to fool our air observers and recon planes.

The 9.Panzer-Division insignia on the rear plate enabled Martin Block to identify the vehicle as one of two Bergepanzer IIIs shipped to the unit in September 1944. One was still present on January 15, 1945. The rudimentary wooden superstructure offered some protection from the elements.

April 10, 1945 (Gasiewicz) (165). Elements of 741st Tank Battalion, 2nd Infantry Regiment, pass through a leveled roadblock in the Altmunded area.

The area is known as Hann. Münden and was passed through by the 2nd Infantry Division and the attached 741st Tank Battalion on their way to Leipzig. Note the gaggle of soldiers watching the progress and the soldier on the back of the M4A3 (76) HVSS, using the telephone; his 2nd ID patch visible.

7TH ARMY PART 2
Riviera to the Rhine

A destroyed Sturmgeschütz III Ausf.F/8 from Pz.Jg.Abt.61, 11.Panzer-Division, tactical number '001'. Note the distinctive 'Gespenster' (ghost) divisional insignia on the bow armor. This vehicle was lost around Baume-les-Dames in September 1944 after the Allied landings in Southern France.

Sturmgeschütz III Ausf.F/8
Pz.Jg.Abt.61, 11.Panzer-Division
Baume-les-Dames, France
September 1944

August 31, 1944 (Bonnard) (163). Street pillbox on turret mounted with 47mm gun and light machine gun built-in commands road along the waterfront. This was used by the Germans in their street defense of Marseilles.

A Somua S35 tank turret being used as a Panzerstellung in the port area of Marseilles. The turret was attached to an underground concrete bunker.

September 25, 1944 (McCroby) (163). Large German troop carrier knocked out along the road Northeast of Besancon. It is being examined by three American soldiers.

This and the next two photos were all taken in sequence. The Sd.Kfz.9, presumably from 11.Panzer-Division, probably belonged to a maintenance unit in an armored regiment and has a spare drive sprocket in the load bed. It is missing the front wheel.

211

September 25, 1944 (McCroby) (163). The burnt remains of a German Tiger tank, which was knocked out along the road Northeast of Besancon, France.

Not a Tiger but a demolished Pz.Kpfw.IV Ausf.H with its turret and superstructure flung in front of the house in the background. It does at least allow the GIs to have a good look around. The date and location make this tank from Pz.Rgt.15, 11.Panzer-Division.

September 25, 1944 (McCroby) (163). The burnt remains of a German Tiger tank, which was knocked out along the road Northeast of Besancon, France.

This view of the Pz.Kpfw.IV shows that the turret had been traversed to the rear when it was blown off. The tank had no tactical number on the turret 'Schürzen' but did have 'Zimmerit.'

December 16, 1944 (Bell) (163). Men and armor of the 14th Armored Division pass a German customs house as they cross the German border for the first time. CCA, 14th Armored Division.

It is unclear exactly where this because the current day border is the Rhine River, and the previous photo in the sequence is near Wissembourg, France. Regardless, the photo shows off the camouflage pattern applied to this 14th Armored Division tank, probably from the 25th Tank Battalion.

February 11, 1945 (Moors) (163). A 105mm howitzer on an M7 chassis is mired in 3 feet of mud. The heavy vehicle is stopped from moving forward but can easily move itself out backward; this is due to the weight at the front overbalancing it. Battery B, 342nd Armored Field Artillery Battalion. Lauterbach, Germany.

The 342nd AFA was a non-divisional artillery unit that converted to the 105mm Howitzer Motor Carriage M7 late in 1943. The vehicle has whitewash remains from the January engagements, supports for a tarpaulin, and is towing a G-518 1-Ton trailer.

February 14, 1945 (Moors) (163). While on a recon mission in the woods, this armored car sunk in the earth made soft by heavy rain and thawing snow. Nearby enemy patrols add to the hazards of digging it out. Co. F, 101st Cavalry Reconnaissance Squadron. Karlsbrunn, Germany.

This Light Armored Car M8 would require a recovery vehicle to extricate it from the mud. Chains on the wheels, while giving more grip, are useless here. The 101st Cavalry Squadron was attached to XV Corps during February 1945.

March 9, 1945 (Bell) (163). 0·50 caliber anti-aircraft machine gun on a new M-24 light tank is fired by Sgt. John Driscoll, of SD, tank commander, on the practice range. Co. F, 117th Cavalry Reconnaissance Squadron, VI Corps. St Jean, Saverne area, France.

The beginning of March saw the 117th turn in their M5 Light Tanks for the Light Tank M24. The AAR report for March 8 and 9 states: "Our new tanks had their first opportunity to fire the 75mm gun. Recommendations for the modifications on the new light tanks have been submitted to the Ordnance personnel."

217

March 16, 1945 (163).

This is Jagdtiger '332' of s.Pz.Jg.Abt.653, knocked out by American fighter-bombers near Morsbronn, France. Jagdtiger '314' was destroyed a short distance from this vehicle.

March 16, 1945 (Rutberg) (163). Tank dozer filling in a crater so that the traffic can move through newly captured Erfweiler. 191st Tank Battalion, 45th Infantry Division.

A Medium Tank Dozer M4, with an interesting camouflage pattern, applied back-fills a crater. The vehicle is based on an M4A1.

March 21, 1945 (Leibowitz) (163). 1st Lt. Richard Keene of Quincy, Mass, a fighter pilot of the 324th Fighter Group, crash-landed his P-47 after a dive-bombing mission in Germany due to a defective prop. He was found by Pfc Russell Rebert, a 7th Army Signal Corpsman. Woerth Area, France.

Thanks to P-47 historian Jon Bernstein, we know that the plane's crash landing on March 21 was its second hard landing in three months. In the first incident, the aircraft had an accident when landing at Lunéville on January 9, 1945, under the controls of Captain Harry Chance. Lt. Keene was with the 315th Fighter Squadron.

March 17, 1945 (Bowen) (163). Tank crew refueling with gasoline before the attack. 756th Tank Battalion, 3rd Infantry Division. Altheim area, France.

The cameraman had this tank further east than it actually was, as Altheim is in Austria near the Danube. This Medium Tank M4A3 (76) HVSS, with a full complement of sandbags for protection, refuels in Alteheim, France.

March 20, 1945 (Newell) (163). A new light tank, M-24, crosses a new bridge built by engineers of the 42nd Infantry Division. Infantry and engineers rush small light bridges to keep up with the rapid movement on this front. Troop F, 117th Cavalry Reconnaissance Squadron, 42nd Infantry, VI Corps. Lembach Forest area, France.

The driver has the windshield erected, indicating that the tank is probably moving at high speed. Interesting markings on the bow that indicate the tank is the 12th vehicle of Troop F, 117th Cavalry Reconnaissance Squadron, VI Corps. Note the size of the 0·50 caliber machine gun compared to the width of the turret.

March 24, 1945 (Newell) (163). M-8 Howitzer in action near Weschnitz, Germany. 12th Armored Division.

The rear of a 75mm Howitzer Motor Carriage M8 in action on a road overlooking the town of Weschnitz. The M8, while lightly armored, was fast and could deliver artillery support quickly.

April 8, 1945 (Blau) (163). Infantrymen loaded on a tank, study the town of Konigshofen through glasses before entering. 2nd Battalion, 180th Infantry Regiment, 45th Infantry Division, 7th Army.

Three Medium Tanks M4A3 (76) HVSS, probably from the 191st Tank Battalion, wait in an open field before entering the town. Bad Königshofen was taken after Aschaffenburg and before the 45th moved towards Nuremberg.

April 11, 1945 (Blau) (163). In the battle for Bamberg, the Germans lost almost two dozen tanks to the 45th Infantry Division, without losing any American tanks. Many of their tanks were well dug in, prepared for a strong defense of the city. 45th Infantry Division, XV Corps, 7th Army. Bamberg, Germany.

Hidden behind a brick wall is this Pz.Kpfw III Ausf.D from Pz.Ersatz- und Ausbildungs-Abteilung 35. A shot through the 14·5mm thick rear armor has disabled the tank, the crew finishing the job with demolition charges - blowing the back of the turret away. With its 3·7cm main weapon, it was a disadvantage compared to anything else on the battlefield.

April 11, 1945 (Blau) (163). German shortage of gasoline has forced conversion even in their armored vehicles. Here are two full-tracked vehicles in the process of having wood burners put on. 45th Infantry Division, XV Corps, 7th Army. Bamberg, Germany.

Both vehicles here are training tanks with wood-gas generators. In the foreground is a Pz.Kpfw.II Ausf.b wanne. The other end of this garage in Bamberg was shown in Panzerwrecks 1, and the vehicles belonged to Pz.Ersatz- und Ausbildungs-Abteilung 35.

April 16, 1945 (Stubenrauch) (163). Doughboys of the 1st Battalion, 232nd Infantry Regiment, 42nd Infantry Division, following the armored thrust by the 12th Armored Division tanks, into the captured town of Neustadt.

GIs move past two Medium Tanks M4A3 (76) HVSS from 43rd Tank Battalion, in Neustadt Town Square, which appears to be in perfect condition. Note the small details on the tank, such as M3 submachine guns on the turret and sandbags held in place with a wooden beam.

The 14th Armored Division was in action around Heidelberg, where they apparently encountered a few Panthers. We were unable to confirm the identity of the unit as we are not aware of any Panthers in the Heidelberg area.

XX CORPS

General Walton Walker Albums

February 27, 1945 (166). Tankers make last-minute checkup before going into action. Saarlautern.

No unit is given, and this rare 90mm Tank Destroyer M36B1 could be from one of several tank destroyer battalions attached to the 3rd Army at this time. The M36B1 saw the standard M36 turret mated to the hull of an M4A3.

March 14, 1945 (Crabtree) (166). Trier. Tank crew cleans tanks machine guns in preparation for the new drive.

After fierce fighting in Trier, this crew takes advantage of the brief rest to clean their weapons and prepare for the next action. The tank is a Medium Tank M4A3 (76).

March 14, 1945 (166). Near Beurig, engineers look over a knocked out American tank caught in a tank trap.

This Medium Tank M4A3 (75) named 'Bold Adventure' from 778th Tank Battalion or 10th Armored Division tried to cross this anti-tank ditch, but was hit in the side by an anti-tank round. Engineers inspect the damage and would need to call a tank retriever up to remove it from the ditch.

March 16, 1945 (Bradley) (166). Serrig, Germany. 90mm shells are loaded aboard an M-36 tank destroyer, and last-minute checks are made before going into action.

Bombing-up. The crew of a 90mm Gun Motor Carriage M36 from the 818th Tank Destroyer Battalion (attached to the 26th Infantry Division) load ammunition after a fire mission. According to the AAR, 'A' Company of the 818th was in Serrig on March 16.

March 18, 1945 (166). Selbruck, Germany. Knocked out German Mark IV tank burns in a field outside Selbruck. Tank and roadblock were used in a vain attempt to halt the armored advance.

The town is actually Selbach, southeast of Hermeskeil. The 10th Armored and 80th Infantry Divisions were both in the area. The 10th Armored Division AAR mentions a burning tank outside of Selbach, and German accounts note that there were two Stugs in a blocking position. After knocking out one US tank, one was destroyed and the second ran out of fuel and was set on fire by its crew.

March 22, 1945 (166). Maxdorf, Germany. American tanks move through the city in preparation for an attack on Ludwigshafen.

A Medium Tank M4A3 (76) of 'A' Company, 3rd Tank Battalion, Team Holland, TF Hankins of the 10th Armored Division, advances through Maxdorf. Two 75mm HMC M8s follow.

XX Corps

CAMERAMEN

In Action

▲ Tec 4 Anthony T. Martin with a young French girl in Normandy, July 1944. Martin was a motion picture cameraman with Detachments A and G of the 165th SPC. Before the war, Martin worked in special effects in Hollywood.

▶ Tec 5 John P. Salis of the 165th SPC. Salis was a cameraman with Detachments A and F of the 165th during the war.

September 18, 1944 (Carolan) (165). Pfc. Josiah Carpenter is a cameraman with the 165th Signal Photo Company and has been with the unit since D+3.

Carpenter, here in a staged photo, was a still cameraman with Detachment A of the 165th Signal Photo Company.

September 18, 1944 (Carolan) (165). Cpl. Robert Leiter is a motion picture cameraman with the 165th Signal Photo Company.

This shot was taken at the same time, with the same Jeep, as the photo above. Leiter worked in a camera store before the war, started as a still photographer before switching to motion pictures. He served with Detachments A and H of the 165th SPC.

January 9, 1945 (Bell) (167th). Sgt. Bernhard Bonwitt is photographed outside his Jeep near Rotgen, Germany.

This Jeep, from the 167th Signal Photo Company, has a steel beam installed on the front to cut barbed wire. It has the markings of a US Army War Photographer on the engine grill and under the windshield, should there be any confusion. Each photo unit seemed to use different markings.

March 19, 1945 (Newell) (163). Cameraman gets his Jeep past a bomb crater near the front around Bitche, France. 7th Army.

It is not clear which member of Newell's team this is, but he is a motion picture cameraman. The Jeep has been painted with 'Official Cameraman' and has a 'Press' sign on the windshield.

April 11, 1945 (Kitzerow) (165). Lt. Don Sykes of Hollywood, CA, looks over burnt German helmets in a railyard in Northeim, Germany.

Lt. Sykes was the leader of Detachment R of the 165th and had been with them since Normandy.

April 27, 1945 (Braun) (165). Tec 5 Fred Poinsett, photographer of the 165th Signal Photo Company, with the crew of a Russian T-34 tank. Torgau, Germany.

Poinsett and his unit partner Ernest Braun were in the Torgau area, photographing the 69th Infantry Division link up with the Russians on the Elbe river. Poinsett holds his Speed Graphic camera.

July 5, 1945 (Hollander) (165). 2nd Lt. Leon Rosenmann loads up his camera while curious Soviet soldiers look on at a roadblock near Tremensdorf, Germany.

Rosenmann was with Detachment K of the 165th SPC, assigned to the 3rd Armored Division. His still photo partner was Joe DeMarco until January 1945. Note his 3rd Armored Division patch even though he was with the 165th SPC.